and Dubious
Achievements

John S. Snyder

CHRONICLE BOOKS
SAN FRANCISCO

Printed in Singapore.

ISBN 0-8118-0560-3
Library of Congress Cataloging-in-Publication Data available.

Book and cover design by Tonya Hudson
Cover illustration by Charlie Powell
Composition by T:H Typecast, Inc.

Distributed in Canada by Raincoast Books,
112 East 3rd Avenue, Vancouver, B.C. V5T 1C8

10 9 8 7 6 5 4 3 2

Chronicle Books
275 Fifth Street
San Francisco, CA 94103

## INTRODUCTION

FOR OVER 150 winters hockey has thrilled and chilled, bumped and bruised, crashed and bashed its players and fans alike. Although the exact beginnings of the game are unknown, most historians agree that the game evolved from "shinny" or "bandy," played by British soldiers stationed in eastern Canada in the 1840s. By the early 1880s the game had developed into one similar to the one we see played today in countless arenas throughout the world.

*Hockey! Great Moments & Dubious Achievements* chronicles the game, capturing its myth and magic with anecdotes as unique and exciting as the game itself. Spend a few minutes and meet the players, coaches, and teams who are remembered for just one shining moment or an entire stellar career, for great success or unbelievable embarrassment, or simply for being the first or last to accomplish their individual feat.

Some achievements, like Bobby Baun's dramatic overtime goal for the Toronto Maple Leafs in the 1964 Stanley Cup finals—scored while playing with a fractured ankle—have singularly ensured a place in hockey lore forever. Other feats represent just one moment in an exemplary career, such as Hall of Famer Bill Mosienko's three goals in 21 seconds—a blink of an eye in a 14-year career with the Chicago Blackhawks.

Sometimes, though, it's best not to be remembered at all. Just ask Vancouver Canuck goaltender Dunc Wilson, who managed to "one up" Mosienko by surrendering three goals to the Boston Bruins in just 20 seconds. Or ask Gary Smith, the California Seals goalie who chalked up a "memorable" record 48 losses in one season.

On the pages of this puck-shaped book you'll find exploits by more than 200 players, coaches, and teams that have happened just once in over a century and a half's history of the world's fastest sport. Quick! The action's just starting!

—Mike Harling, Vancouver, 1994

Author's note: The records in *Hockey!* include those of the National Hockey League (NHL), World Hockey Association (WHA), and the Stanley Cup. The NHL has been in operation continually since the 1917-18 season. The WHA existed from the 1972-73 season through the 1978-79 season. The Stanley Cup has been the symbol of hockey supremacy since it was inaugurated in 1893. The NHL competed with the Pacific Coast Hockey Association and the Western Canada Hockey League for the Cup from the 1917-18 season through the 1925-26 season. The Western leagues disbanded after 1926, and the NHL has competed exclusively since then.

## Jack Adams

THE ONLY COACH whose team won a game by 15 goals.

The Detroit Red Wings, under coach Jack Adams, routed the New York Rangers 15-0 on January 23, 1944, in Detroit in the most lopsided game in NHL history. The Red Wings scored two goals in the first period, five in the second, and eight in the third against hapless Ranger goalie Ken (Tubby) McAuley. So thorough was the rout that Detroit outshot New York 58-9 and 10 different Red Wings scored goals. Syd Howe led the way with three goals and Joe Carveth had four assists.

## Wendell Anderson

THE ONLY SITTING state governor to be drafted by a major league hockey club.

Minnesota Governor Wendell Anderson was 36 years old and a former member of the U.S. National Team when he was drafted by the Minnesota Fighting Saints in the first World Hockey Association draft in 1972. Anderson decided to forgo the opportunity to play pro hockey and kept his day job.

## Al Arbour

THE ONLY INDIVIDUAL to coach more than 1,500 regular-season NHL games.

Through the 1992-93 season, Al Arbour had been behind the bench in 1,522 games with the St. Louis Blues (1970-73) and the New York Islanders (1973-86 and 1988-93). Arbour's record is 745-541-236. He was the coach of Stanley Cup champions with the Islanders in 1979-80, 1980-81, 1981-82, and 1982-83.

## PETE BABANDO

THE ONLY PLAYER to score a double-overtime goal in game seven of a Stanley Cup final.

Pete Babando of the Detroit Red Wings scored only six goals during the 1949-50 season, but was the hero in the Stanley Cup final. The Red Wings and the New York Rangers squared off for the deciding seventh game of the 1950 Stanley Cup final on April 23 in Detroit. Ending the longest seventh game in finals history, Babando scored the winning goal at 28:31 of overtime to give Detroit the championship with a 4-3 win.

## BILL BARILKO

THE ONLY PLAYER to die in a plane crash shortly after scoring a Stanley Cup-clinching overtime goal.

Bill Barilko scored only 26 regular-season goals in a five-year NHL career, but he became a hero on April 21, 1951, when he scored a goal at 2:53 of overtime in game five of the Stanley Cup final to give the Toronto Maple Leafs a 3-2 win over the Montreal Canadiens and the championship. A few months later, however, Barilko died in a plane crash en route to a fishing trip in northern Ontario.

## Bobby Baun

THE ONLY PLAYER to score an overtime goal in a Stanley Cup final while playing on a fractured ankle.

In the third period of the sixth game of the Stanley Cup final on April 23, 1964, between the Toronto Maple Leafs and the Red Wings in Detroit, Bobby Baun of Toronto was felled with an injured ankle and had to be removed on a stretcher. He returned and scored a goal at 1:43 of overtime, which gave the Maple Leafs a 4-3 win and evened the series at three games apiece. After the series was over, Baun finally consented to have the ankle x-rayed, and learned it was fractured.

## Don Beaupre and Eddie Mio

THE ONLY TWO goaltenders to allow three goals in 15 seconds.

The three fastest goals in NHL history were scored on Don Beaupre of the Minnesota North Stars and Eddie Mio of the New York Rangers on February 10, 1983, in Minnesota in a 15-second span of the second period. Mark Pavelich of the Rangers struck first at 19:18 and was followed by teammate Ron Greschner at 19:27. Will Plett scored for the North Stars at 19:33. Minnesota won the game 7-5.

## Clint Benedict

THE ONLY GOALTENDER with 15 shutouts in play-off competition.

Clint Benedict still holds the record for most shutouts in play-off competition, which he accomplished between 1917 and 1930 with the Ottawa Senators and Montreal Maroons. Benedict is also the first goalie to wear a mask, which he introduced on February 20, 1930, with Montreal. He donned the mask to protect his broken nose, but the mask came loose during a game later in the season, causing him to break his nose again. The injury forced him to retire.

## Max Bentley

THE ONLY PLAYER to score four goals and an assist in one period.

Max Bentley scored four goals and had an assist for the Chicago Blackhawks on January 28, 1943, in the third period of a 10-1 rout of the New York Rangers in Chicago. Max's brother Doug assisted on all four goals and was simply returning a favor. Doug had scored a goal in the first period and another in the second on assists by Max.

## Red Berenson

THE ONLY PLAYER to score six goals in a road game.

Red Berenson is one of only seven NHL players to score at least six goals in a game, one of only three to do it since 1921, and the only one to net six in a road game. He accomplished the feat with the St. Louis Blues on November 7, 1968, in an 8-0 win over the Flyers at the Spectrum in Philadelphia. Berenson scored one in the first period, four in the second, and one in the third.

## TOE BLAKE

THE ONLY COACH to win five consecutive Stanley Cup championships.

Toe Blake won five consecutive Stanley Cup championships with the Montreal Canadiens from 1955-56 through 1959-60, and he did it in his first five seasons as coach. He also holds the record for most total championships won by a coach with eight. The others were in 1964-65, in 1965-66, and in his last season as coach in 1967-68. Blake's record in the Stanley Cup finals was 32-10.

## Gus Bodnar

THE ONLY PLAYER to score a goal 15 seconds after face-off in his first NHL game.

Gus Bodnar scored the fastest goal in NHL history by a player in his first game on October 30, 1943, for the Maple Leafs against the New York Rangers in Toronto. He scored at 0:15 of the first period and again at 1:41 of the third in Toronto's 5-2 win. Bodnar, who turned 18 only two months before his smashing debut, went on to have a 12-year career in the NHL.

## Mike Bossy

THE ONLY PLAYER to score at least 50 goals nine seasons in a row.

Mike Bossy scored 53 goals as a rookie with the New York Islanders in 1977-78, the first of an NHL record nine consecutive seasons of at least 50 goals. Bossy's goal totals over the next eight seasons were 69, 51, 68, 64, 60, 51, 58, and 61. His 83 assists in 1981-82 are also a record by a right wing. Bossy was forced to give up the game after the 1986-87 season, in which he scored 38 goals, due to a painful lower-back ailment.

## Boston Bruins

THE ONLY TEAM to sweep a four-game Stanley Cup final series by 13 goals.

The most one-sided Stanley Cup final in history was the one in 1970 when the Boston Bruins swept the St. Louis Blues four straight by scores of 6-1 and 6-2 in St. Louis and 4-1 and 4-3 in Boston. The Bruins were led by stars such as Bobby Orr, Phil Esposito, Ken Hodge, John Bucyk, Wayne Cashman, John McKenzie, Gerry Cheevers, Ed Westfall, Dallas Smith, and Derek Sanderson under coach Harry Sinden.

## Frank Boucher

THE ONLY PLAYER to win the Lady Byng Trophy seven times.

As a right wing with the New York Rangers, Frank Boucher won the Lady Byng Trophy, awarded annually to the player "adjudged to have exhibited the best type of sportsmanship and gentlemanly conduct combined with a high standard of playing ability," a record seven times. Boucher won the award in 1927-28, 1928-29, 1929-30, 1930-31, 1932-33, 1933-34, and 1934-35. He was also runner-up in 1931-32. After he won the award the seventh time, Boucher was given permanent possession of the trophy, which was replaced by a new one.

## Ray Bourque

THE ONLY DEFENSEMAN to be named a first- or second-team NHL All-Star 14 times.

Boston Bruins defenseman Ray Bourque played in his 14th NHL season in 1992-93 and was named a first-team All-Star for the 10th time. He has also been selected to the second-team on four occasions, which means he has been an All-Star every season beginning with his rookie campaign in 1979-80.

## Johnny Bower

THE OLDEST PLAYER to tend goal in a Stanley Cup game.

Johnny Bower became the oldest goaltender in Stanley Cup history on April 6, 1969, while playing for the Toronto Maple Leafs in a 3-2 loss to the Boston Bruins in the quarterfinals at Maple Leaf Gardens. He was 44 years, four months, and 28 days old. Bower played in only one more game, during the 1969-70 regular season, before retiring.

## Scotty Bowman

THE ONLY COACH with more than 800 regular-season wins.

Through the 1992-93 season, Scotty Bowman has a record 834 regular-season wins with the St. Louis Blues (1967-71), Montreal Canadiens (1971-79), Buffalo Sabres (1979-87), and Pittsburgh Penguins (1991-93). His record is 834-380-226. Bowman also holds the record for most play-off wins with 137. He was the coach of Stanley Cup champs in Montreal in 1972-73, 1975-76, 1976-77, 1977-78, and 1978-79, and in Pittsburgh in 1991-92. Bowman's 1976-77 Canadiens were 60-8-12 in the regular season to earn a record 132 points.

## FRANKIE BRIMSEK

THE ONLY GOALTENDER to record six shutouts in his first eight NHL games.

Frankie Brimsek earned the nickname "Mr. Zero" by posting a shutout in six of his first eight NHL games with the Boston Bruins. Brimsek debuted on December 1, 1938, and lost to the Canadiens 2-0 in Montreal, but shut out the Chicago Blackhawks 5-0 on December 4, Chicago again 2-0 on December 6, and the New York Rangers 2-0 on December 11. After a 3-2 win against Montreal on December 13, Brimsek shut out three more opponents in succession.

## Harry "Punch" Broadbent

THE ONLY PLAYER to score a goal in more than 14 consecutive games.

Harry "Punch" Broadbent scored in 16 consecutive games for the Ottawa Senators in 1921-22, a streak in which he scored 25 goals. In the 1921-22 season, Broadbent had 32 goals in 24 games.

## WALTER "TURK" BRODA

THE ONLY GOALTENDER to play in at least 60 play-off games and compile a goals-against average under 2.00.

Walter "Turk" Broda was a tough customer in the nets for the Toronto Maple Leafs between 1936 and 1952. He played in 102 play-off games and had a goals-against average of 1.98 goals per game. Broda's performance helped Toronto win the Stanley Cup in 1941-42, 1946-47, 1947-48, 1948-49, and 1950-51.

## John Bucyk

THE ONLY LEFT wing to score more than 1,200 points in the NHL.

John Bucyk holds the record for most points by a left wing in the NHL with 1,369 on 556 goals and 813 assists. Bobby Hull is second with 1,170 points. Bucyk's 813 assists is also a record by a left wing. He played with the Detroit Red Wings in 1955-56 and 1956-57 and the Boston Bruins from 1957-58 through 1977-78. His season high was 116 points (51 goals, 65 assists) in 1970-71.

## BUFFALO SABRES

THE ONLY TEAM to score nine goals in one period.

The Buffalo Sabres scored an NHL record nine goals in one period in a 14-4 rout of the Toronto Maple Leafs on March 19, 1981. Buffalo led 1-0 at the end of the first period before their nine-goal onslaught in the second period on Toronto goaltender Michel Larocque. Three of the nine goals were scored by Gil Perreault, two by Andre Savard, and the rest by Derek Smith, Ric Seiling, Craig Ramsay, and Danny Gare.

## John Brophy

THE ONLY COACH whose club made the Stanley Cup play-offs despite a winning percentage of less than .350.

The 1987-88 Toronto Maple Leafs, under coach John Brophy, qualify as the worst team in NHL history to reach the play-offs. Toronto was 21-49-10 in the regular season for a winning percentage of .325. In the play-offs, the Maple Leafs lost a best-of-seven series to the Detroit Red Wings in six games.

## Mud Bruneteau

THE ONLY PLAYER to score a goal in the longest game in NHL history.

The Detroit Red Wings and the Montreal Maroons opened their best-of-five play-off series on March 24, 1936, in Montreal with the longest game in NHL history. It lasted 176 minutes, 30 seconds, before Mud Bruneteau of the Red Wings scored on a pass from Hec Kilrea past Montreal goaltender Lorne Chabot at 2:20 a.m., to give Detroit a 1-0 win. It was only the third goal of Bruneteau's NHL career. Norm Smith was the Red Wings goaltender credited with the longest shutout performance. Detroit went on to sweep the series.

## Calgary Flames

THE ONLY TEAM to go 264 consecutive regular-season games without being shut out.

The Calgary Flames scored at least one goal in every regular-season game between November 12, 1981, and January 9, 1985, an NHL record streak of 264 games. It ended on January 10, when the Nordiques and goalie Richard Sevigny stopped the Flames 4-0 in Quebec.

## Paul Cavallini

THE ONLY PLAYER to have the tip of his finger auctioned for charity.

In a game against the Chicago Blackhawks on December 22, 1990, in St. Louis, Blues defenseman Paul Cavallini lost the tip of his finger when he was struck by a slap shot off the stick of Chicago's Doug Wilson. A St. Louis radio announcer gained possession of the severed digit after it was stolen by a clerk in the pathology department at the hospital where Cavallini was treated. The radio announcer then came up with the bright idea of auctioning off the tip for charity but Cavallini protested.

## Guy Charron

THE ONLY PLAYER to appear in over 700 regular-season games without ever playing in a play-off game.

Guy Charron was good enough in a 12-year NHL career to play in 734 regular-season games, score 221 goals, and accumulate 530 points, but he never played in a play-off game. Charron broke in with the Montreal Canadiens in 1969-70, but that was the only season in the last 45 years that the Canadiens missed the play-offs. He also played for the Detroit Red Wings from 1970-71 to 1974-75, with the Kansas City Scouts in 1974-75 and 1975-76, and the Washington Capitals from 1976-77 to 1980-81.

## Gerry Cheevers

THE ONLY GOALTENDER to go undefeated for 32 consecutive games.

Gerry Cheevers put together the longest undefeated streak by a goaltender in NHL history with the Boston Bruins in 1971-72. He was unbeaten for 32 consecutive games with 24 wins and eight ties.

## DON CHERRY

THE ONLY COACH whose club had eleven 20-goal scorers.

The 1977-78 Boston Bruins under coach Don Cherry are the only team in NHL history with eleven 20-goal scorers. The balanced offense featured Peter McNab (41 goals), Terry O'Reilly (29), Bobby Schmautz (27), Stan Jonathan (27), Jean Ratelle (25), Rick Middleton (25), Wayne Cashman (24), Gregg Sheppard (23), Brad Park (22), Don Marcotte (20), and Bob Miller (20). The Bruins posted a 51-18-11 record and made it to the Stanley Cup finals, before losing in six games to the Montreal Canadiens.

## CHICAGO BLACKHAWKS

THE ONLY NHL team with a regular-season winning percentage worse than .475 to win the Stanley Cup.

The 1937-38 Chicago Blackhawks had a regular season of 14-25-9 for a winning percentage of .385, but won the Stanley Cup. In the first series, a best of three against the Montreal Canadiens, the Blackhawks lost the first game, won the second, and were trailing 2-1 in the third before winning in overtime. In the semifinals, versus the New York Americans, Chicago again lost the first game before winning the series. In the final, they beat the Toronto Maple Leafs three games to one to take the title.

## Dino Ciccarelli

THE ONLY ROOKIE to earn more than 20 points in an NHL play-off season.

Dino Ciccarelli made quite an impact as a rookie with the Minnesota North Stars in the 1980-81 Stanley Cup play-offs. After totaling just 30 points during the regular season on 18 goals and 12 assists, Ciccarelli set an NHL play-off record for most points by a rookie with 21 on 14 goals and 7 assists. The North Stars lost in the finals in five games to the New York Islanders.

## King Clancy

THE ONLY INDIVIDUAL to play at all six positions in a Stanley Cup game.

Hall of Famer King Clancy played all six positions for the Ottawa Senators in a 1-0 win over the Western Canada Hockey League champion Edmonton Eskimos on March 31, 1923, in Vancouver. Clancy played on both sides of the defense, at center, and on both wings, and took a two-minute turn in goal when Ottawa goaltender Clint Benedict was penalized for slashing. The win clinched the Stanley Cup championship for Ottawa.

## Monte Clark

THE ONLY FORMER NFL coach to break up a fight between two NHL coaches.

Two months after he was fired by the National Football League Detroit Lions, Monte Clark took in an NHL game in Detroit between the Red Wings and the Minnesota North Stars on February 14, 1985. At the end of the first period, a bench-clearing brawl erupted which included a five-minute wrestling match between the two coaches, Nick Polano of the Red Wings and Glen Sonmor of the North Stars. Clark left his seat near the Red Wings bench and pulled Polano out of the fracas and escorted him to the dressing room. The contest ended in a 5-5 tie.

## Paul Coffey

THE ONLY DEFENSEMAN with more than 310 career goals.

Through the 1992-93 season, Paul Coffey held the career record for most goals (330) and most assists (871) by a defenseman. Coffey also holds the single-season record for goals by a defenseman with 48 for the Edmonton Oilers in 1985-86. He played on three Stanley Cup champions with Edmonton and one with the Pittsburgh Penguins.

## ALEX CONNELL

THE ONLY GOALTENDER to post six consecutive shutouts.

Alex Connell of the Ottawa Senators posted six consecutive shutouts in 1927-28. Over eight games, he shut out the opposition for 461 minutes, 29 seconds.

## BILLY COUTURE

THE ONLY PLAYER to be suspended for life by the NHL for assaulting referees.

The play of Billy Couture was so violent that during the 1923 play-offs as a member of the Montreal Canadiens, he was suspended by team owner Leo Dandurand for brutality on the ice. In 1927 while with the Boston Bruins, Couture became angry after a 3-1 loss to the Ottawa Senators which eliminated the Bruins, and attacked referees Gerry LaFlamme and Billy Bell. For his actions, Couture was suspended for life by the NHL.

# TERRY CRISP

THE ONLY COACH whose team scored two short-handed goals in four seconds.

Terry Crisp's Calgary Flames put together a stirring comeback on October 17, 1989, against the Quebec Nordiques to come away with an 8-8 tie. The Flames trailed 8-3 with less than seven minutes remaining when they scored three goals in a 27-second span in the third period. The cause still looked hopeless with 19 seconds left and the short-handed Flames losing 8-6. But goals by Doug Gilmour at 19:45 and Paul Ranheim at 19:49 tied the contest at 8-8.

## LES CUNNINGHAM

THE ONLY PLAYER with fewer than 30 points in a career to total five in one period.

Only 10 players in NHL history have been credited with five points in one period. One of them is Les Cunningham, who had only 26 points on seven goals and 19 assists in his entire career. Cunningham broke loose with two goals and three assists in the third period for the Chicago Blackhawks on January 28, 1940, against the Montreal Canadiens in Chicago in an 8-1 win. Chicago scored six goals in the period.

## Pete and Jerry Cusimano

THE ONLY PAIR of brothers to start a tradition of octopus throwing.

The Detroit Red Wings had won seven straight play-off games when they took the ice against the Montreal Canadiens in Detroit on April 15, 1952, with a chance to win the Stanley Cup. Pete and Jerry Cusimano, whose father worked in the fish business, decided to throw an octopus onto the ice before the game because the eight-legged creature signified the eight play-off wins necessary to win the Cup. The Red Wings won 3-0, and a tradition was born. Fans to this day continue to throw octopuses onto the ice before Red Wing home play-off games.

## Dawson City Klondikers

THE ONLY TEAM to lose a Stanley Cup match by 21 goals.

Dawson City from the Yukon Territory challenged the Ottawa Silver Seven for the Stanley Cup in 1905, but lost the best-of-three series by 9-2 on January 13 and 23-2 on January 16. It's no wonder after what the Dawson City team had to endure to reach Ottawa, 4,400 miles away. They traveled 400 miles to Skagway, Alaska, by dogsled and on foot in temperatures as low as 20 below. After a five-day layover, they traveled to Seattle on one boat and to Vancouver on another before making a cross-country train trip to Ottawa. The trek took 23 days.

## Clarence "Hap" Day

THE ONLY COACH to win a Stanley Cup final after trailing three games to none.

Clarence "Hap" Day's Toronto Maple Leafs were in a precarious position in the 1942 Stanley Cup final against the Detroit Red Wings. They trailed three games to none after losing 3-2 and 4-2 in Toronto and 5-2 in Detroit. But the Maple Leafs rallied in incredible fashion. In game four in Detroit, the Maple Leafs trailed 2-0 in the first period and 3-2 in the third before winning 4-3. Toronto won the next three, 9-3 at home, 3-0 in Detroit, and 3-1 back in Toronto to take the series and the championship.

## Alex Delvecchio

THE ONLY PLAYER with a career lasting longer than 1,400 games to play on only one team.

Alex Delvecchio is the only player to appear in more than 1,400 games in the NHL without playing on more than one team. He was in 1,549 regular-season games with the Detroit Red Wings between 1950 and 1974. Long one-team careers are rather rare in the NHL. Of the 23 players to appear in at least 1,200 regular-season games, only three played with one team. The other two, besides Delvecchio, are Stan Mikita (Chicago) and Henri Richard (Montreal).

## Jacques Demers

THE ONLY COACH to win 10 overtime play-off games in one year.

The Montreal Canadiens, under coach Jacques Demers, opened the 1993 play-offs with a 3-2 overtime loss to the Quebec Nordiques. The Canadiens played 10 more overtime games in the play-offs, and won them all. They had two overtime wins in a six-game series against Quebec, won three in overtime in a four-game sweep of the Buffalo Sabres, and had two more in a 4-1 series win over the New York Islanders. In the final, Montreal won three times in overtime against the Los Angeles Kings to capture the Stanley Cup in a five-game series.

## Cy Denneny

THE ONLY PLAYER to finish second in the NHL scoring race six times.

Cy Denneny of the Ottawa Senators led the NHL in scoring in 1923-24 with 22 goals and one assist, but couldn't do it again, as he finished second six times to five different players. Denneny was second to Joe Malone in 1917-18, to Newsy Lalonde in 1920-21, to Punch Broadbent in 1921-22, to Babe Dye in both 1922-23 and 1924-25, and to Nels Stewart in 1925-26. Denneny also finished third in the scoring race in both 1918-19 and 1919-20.

## Eric DesJardins

THE ONLY DEFENSEMAN to score a hat trick in a Stanley Cup final.

Eric DesJardins not only became the only defenseman to score a hat trick in a Stanley Cup final, but provided the Montreal Canadiens with all three of its goals in a 3-2 triumph over the Los Angeles Kings on June 3, 1993, in Montreal. DesJardins, who had only 13 goals during the regular season, tied the contest 2-2 with 73 seconds left in regulation. The Canadiens had a man advantage at the time because Marty McSorley of the Kings was given a penalty for having an illegal curve in his stick. DesJardins scored the game winner after 51 seconds of overtime.

## Detroit Red Wings

THE ONLY FRANCHISE to finish with the best record in the NHL seven consecutive seasons.

The Detroit Red Wings finished first in the six-team NHL for seven consecutive seasons from 1948-49 through 1954-55. The Red Wings had some trouble in the Stanley Cup play-offs, however, winning just four of those years, in 1949-50, 1951-52, 1953-54, and 1954-55. They lost in the final in 1948-49 and the semifinals in 1950-51 and 1952-53. Tommy Ivan coached the team during the first six years of the first-place streak and was succeeded by Jimmy Skinner in 1954-55.

## Marcel Dionne

THE ONLY PLAYER to score over 700 regular-season goals without ever playing in a Stanley Cup final.

Marcel Dionne scored 731 career goals, third highest in NHL history behind Gordie Howe and Wayne Gretzky, but he never had the opportunity to score in a Stanley Cup final. Dionne played for the Detroit Red Wings from 1971-72 through 1974-75, the Los Angeles Kings from 1975-76 through 1986-87, and the New York Rangers from 1986-87 until his retirement after the 1988-89 season. The closest Dionne got to the final was in 1981-82 when the Kings lost the division final.

## KEN DORATY

THE ONLY PLAYER to end a play-off series with a goal in the sixth overtime.

The Boston Bruins and Toronto Maple Leafs battled through 60 minutes of regulation and five overtime periods in the fifth and deciding game of their semifinal play-off series on April 3, 1933, in Toronto without either side denting the goal. The Boston Bruin and Maple Leaf players agreed to end the game with a coin flip to decide the winner, but the Toronto crowd booed lustily and the Maple Leafs backed out of the agreement. At 4:46 of the overtime, number six, Ken Doraty of the Maple Leafs, scored to give Toronto a 1-0 win.

## KEN DRYDEN

THE ONLY GOALTENDER with at least 200 career wins and a winning percentage above .700.

Ken Dryden had a sterling career in goal for the Montreal Canadiens from 1970 through 1979 (though he missed the 1973-74 season to attend law school). He had a record of 258-57-74 for a winning percentage of .758. His goals-against average was 2.24. Dryden played on six Stanley Cup champions and was a first-team All-Star five times in just seven seasons as a regular goaltender.

## RICK DUDLEY

THE ONLY COACH whose team played 24 overtime games during the regular season.

Rick Dudley's Buffalo Sabres played 24 overtime games during the regular season in 1990-91. They had a 3-2-19 record in overtime and were 31-30-19 overall. Buffalo also played one overtime game in the play-offs, a 4-3 loss to the Montreal Canadiens.

## DICK DUFF

THE ONLY PLAYER to score two goals in the first one minute and eight seconds of a play-off game.

Dick Duff scored the Stanley Cup-winning goal for the Toronto Maple Leafs in 1962 against the Chicago Blackhawks at 14:14 of the third period of the sixth game to give Toronto a 2-1 win. In the 1963 series, Duff wasted no time in playing hero again. In the opening game of the play-offs on April 9 against the Detroit Red Wings in Toronto, he scored goals at 0:49 and 1:08 of the first period in the Maple Leafs 4-2 win. Toronto went from there to win the Stanley Cup again.

## Mervyn "Red" Dutton

THE ONLY INDIVIDUAL to play in the NHL after having spent 14 months with his leg in traction from a war wound.

During World War I, Mervyn "Red" Dutton was wounded by exploding shrapnel, which filled his body with 48 fragments of metal and badly mangled his leg. Dutton talked doctors out of amputating his leg and spent 14 months recovering with his leg hoisted at a 30-degree angle. Dutton gained enough strength in the leg to play in the NHL from 1926 through 1936 with the Montreal Maroons and the New York Americans. From 1943 through 1946, Dutton served as president of the NHL.

## Babe Dye

THE ONLY NHL player to score nine goals in a Stanley Cup final.

Babe Dye still holds the NHL record for most goals in a Stanley Cup final. He scored nine for the Toronto St. Patricks in 1922 in a three-games-to-two series win over the Vancouver Millionaires.

## EDDIE EMBERG

THE ONLY PLAYER to score a play-off goal without ever appearing in a regular-season game.

Eddie Emberg's NHL career consisted of two play-off games for the Montreal Canadiens in the 1944-45 play-offs against the Toronto Maple Leafs. He scored in the fifth game of the series, on March 29 at Montreal at 6:02 of the first period in a 10-3 Canadien win. Montreal lost the best-of-seven series in six games.

## PHIL ESPOSITO

THE ONLY PLAYER to take more than 425 shots on goal in a season.

Phil Esposito took an incredible 550 shots on goal with the Boston Bruins in 1970-71, which broke the record of 414, set by Bobby Hull in 1968-69. Esposito scored 76 goals, at a time when the NHL record was Hull's 58. In 1971-72, Esposito scored 66 times on 426 shots. His career total of 717 goals is fourth all-time behind Gordie Howe, Wayne Gretzky, and Marcel Dionne.

## Tony Esposito

THE ONLY GOALTENDER since 1930 to record 15 shutouts in a season.

Playing in 76 games for the Chicago Blackhawks in 1969-70, Tony Esposito recorded 15 shutouts. He had 76 regular-season and 6 play-off shutouts in his career.

## Doug Favell

THE ONLY GOALTENDER to allow a goal that eliminated his team from the play-offs in the last four seconds of the final regular-season game.

The 1971-72 Philadelphia Flyers needed a win or a tie in their final regular-season game on April 2 against the Sabres in Buffalo in order to make it to the play-offs. The Flyers and Sabres were tied 2-2 with four seconds remaining when Gerry Meehan of Buffalo scored on a 30-foot shot past Philadelphia goaltender Doug Favell. The 3-2 Sabre win disqualified the Flyers from the play-offs, but Philadelphia did not miss them again until 1989-90.

## Jack Forbes and Roy "Shrimp" Worters

THE ONLY OPPOSING goaltenders to face 141 shots in a regular-season game.

The New York Americans and Pittsburgh Pirates took 141 shots on goal, the most ever in an NHL regular-season game, on December 26, 1925, in a 3-1 Americans win at Madison Square Garden. Pittsburgh goalie Roy "Shrimp" Worters, who stood only five-feet, three inches, faced 73 shots. Jake Forbes of the Americans had 68 shots fired at him, and stopped all but one.

## Chuck Gardiner

THE ONLY GOALTENDER with a double-overtime shutout in a Stanley Cup final.

Chuck Gardiner was in goal for the Chicago Blackhawks in the only double-overtime shutout in a Stanley Cup final. It came on April 10, 1934, in Chicago against the Detroit Red Wings and gave Chicago the championship. The Blackhawks won the best-of-five series 3-1. The issue was settled when Mush March scored the game's lone goal at 30:05 of overtime. It was to be Chuck Gardiner's last game. Two months later, he died of a brain hemorrhage at the age of 29.

## Herb Gardiner

THE ONLY COACH whose team averaged under one goal per game.

In a dubious record which likely will never be broken, the 1928-29 Chicago Blackhawks averaged under one goal per game with coach Herb Gardiner. Chicago scored only 33 times in 44 games in compiling a 7-29-8 record.

## Mike Gartner

THE ONLY PLAYER to score 30 or more goals for 14 consecutive seasons.

Mike Gartner entered the 1993-94 season with a record 14 consecutive seasons of 30 or more goals. He played with the Washington Capitals from 1979-80 through 1988-89, the Minnesota North Stars in 1988-89 and 1989-90, and the New York Rangers from 1989-90 through 1992-93. His goal totals during those 14 seasons ranged from a low of 33 in 1988-89 to a high of 50 in 1984-85.

## Tommy Gorman

THE ONLY COACH to win back-to-back Stanley Cups with different teams.

Tommy Gorman became the only individual to coach back-to-back Stanley Cup champions with different teams—with the Chicago Blackhawks in 1933-34 and the Montreal Maroons in 1934-35.

## Michel Goulet

THE ONLY LEFT wing to score at least 55 goals in a season three times.

Michel Goulet pumped in 57 goals for the Quebec Nordiques in 1982-83, 56 in 1983-84, and 55 in 1984-85 to become the only left wing to score at least 55 goals in a season three times. He nearly did it a fourth with 53 in 1985-86.

## Wayne Gretzky

THE ONLY PLAYER with more than 86 goals in a season.

Wayne Gretzky began rewriting the NHL record book almost from the moment he entered the league with the Edmonton Oilers in 1979. He shattered the league record for goals in a season with 92 in 1981-82, and had 87 more in 1983-84. Gretzky also holds records for assists in a season (163 in 1985-86), points in a season (215 in 1985-86), hat tricks in a season (10 in 1981-82 and 1983-84), 100-point seasons (13), 40-goal seasons (12), assists in a career (1,563 through the 1992-93 season), and points in a career (2,328 through 1992-93).

## Don Grosso

THE ONLY LEFT wing with six assists in a game.

Don Grosso of the Detroit Red Wings set the single-game assist record for left wings on February 3, 1944, against the New York Rangers in Detroit. Grosso was credited with an assist on all five goals scored by Syd Howe in the 12-2 pasting of the Rangers.

## ARMAND "BEP" GUIDOLIN

THE ONLY 16-year-old to play in the NHL.

Armand "Bep" Guidolin became the youngest player in NHL history when he debuted with the Boston Bruins on November 12, 1942, a month prior to his 17th birthday, in a 3-1 loss to the Maple Leafs in Toronto. Guidolin played nine years in the league with the Bruins, Detroit Red Wings, and Chicago Blackhawks. Harry "Apple Cheeks" Lumley is the youngest goaltender in NHL annals. He was 17 in his first game in 1943 with the Detroit Red Wings. Lumley had a 17-year NHL career, playing for each of the "original" six clubs except Montreal.

## George Hainsworth

THE ONLY GOALTENDER with more than 15 shutouts in a season.

George Hainsworth holds the record for most shutouts in a season by a wide margin. He had 22 for the Montreal Canadiens in 1928-29, seven more than anyone else in league history. And Hainsworth accomplished the feat in a 44-game season. He allowed just 43 goals in those 44 games. He ended his career with 94 shutouts.

## Glenn Hall

THE ONLY GOALTENDER to play in 502 consecutive complete regular-season games.

Glenn Hall played in 502 consecutive regular-season games from the start of the 1955-56 season through November 7, 1962. The streak covered 552 games and 33,135 minutes if the play-offs are counted. He played with the Detroit Red Wings from 1955 through 1957 and the Chicago Blackhawks from 1957 through 1962 during his iron-man stint. Hall's streak ended when he took himself out of a game against the Boston Bruins at 10:21 of the first period because of a pinched nerve in his back.

## HAMILTON TIGERS

THE ONLY NHL team to finish in first place during the regular season and fail to compete in the Stanley Cup play-offs.

The Hamilton Tigers finished the 1924-25 regular season in first place with a record of 19-10-1, but didn't compete in the Stanley Cup play-offs because the players went on strike. Each of the Hamilton players demanded an extra $200 to play in the play-offs. NHL president Frank Calder suspended the players and fined them $200 each and declared that the winner of the series between the second- and third-place teams would represent the NHL in the Stanley Cup final against the Victoria Cougars of the WCHL.

## DALE HAWERCHUK

THE ONLY PLAYER with five assists in one period.

Dale Hawerchuk became the only player to assist on five goals in one period for the Winnipeg Jets against the Kings in Los Angeles on March 6, 1984. Hawerchuk's record performance came in the second period as he contributed to two goals by Morris Lukowich, two by Paul MacLean, and one by Wade Campbell. The Jets won 7-3. Hawerchuk is also the youngest player to score at least 100 points in a season, which he accomplished for Winnipeg in 1981-82. His 100th point came a month before his 19th birthday.

## Ron Hextall

THE ONLY GOALTENDER to shoot the puck into the opposing team's net.

Not only is Ron Hextall of the Philadelphia Flyers the only goalie to shoot a puck into the opposing team's net, but he's done it twice. The first was on December 8, 1987, in a 5-2 win over the Boston Bruins. Hextall retrieved the puck near the right face-off circle and shot it down the ice into an empty net. The second time was in the play-offs against the Washington Capitals on April 11, 1989, when Hextall stopped the puck behind the net, skated to the goal line, and again shot the length of the rink into an empty net in Philadelphia's 8-5 win.

## Al Hill

THE ONLY PLAYER with five points in his first NHL game.

Al Hill burst into the NHL with the Flyers on February 14, 1977, with two goals and three assists in his first game, a 6-4 win over the St. Louis Blues in Philadelphia. He scored on his first two shots, the first one coming after only 35 seconds of play on a 45-foot shot. Hill scored another goal at 11:33 of the second period and had one assist in each period. He played eight more games in 1976-77, but had no more goals and just one assist. Hill didn't score his third career goal until the 1978-79 season, and had just 40 in a 221-game career.

## MEL HILL

THE ONLY PLAYER with three overtime goals in one Stanley Cup series.

Before the 1939 Stanley Cup play-off series between the Boston Bruins and New York Rangers began, Mel Hill was an obscure Bruin right wing with only 12 career goals. By the time the series ended, Hill was part of NHL folklore. He scored three overtime goals. The first two came in the first two games of the best-of-seven series. Boston won the first three games of the series and New York was victorious in the next three. In the seventh and deciding game, Hill scored after 48:00 of overtime and the Bruins took the series with a 2-1 win.

## HARRY "HAP" HOLMES

THE ONLY GOALTENDER to play
on four different Stanley Cup champions.

Harry "Hap" Holmes became the only goaltender to play on four different Stanley Cup champions as a member of the 1914 Toronto Blueshirts, the 1917 Seattle Metropolitans, the 1918 Toronto Arenas, and the 1925 Victoria Cougars.

## RANDY HOLT

THE ONLY PLAYER to be assessed with more than 55 minutes in penalties in one game.

Randy Holt of the Los Angeles Kings not only set an NHL record for most penalty minutes in a game against the Philadelphia Flyers on March 11, 1979, but did it in the first period. By the end of the first 20 minutes of action, Holt already totaled 67 minutes in penalties on one minor, three majors, two 10-minute misconducts, and three game misconducts. The Flyers won the game, played in Philadelphia, 6-3.

## RED HORNER

THE ONLY PLAYER to lead the NHL in penalty minutes eight consecutive seasons.

A rugged defenseman for the Toronto Maple Leafs, Red Horner led the NHL in penalty minutes for eight consecutive seasons from 1932-33 through 1939-40. Horner's penalty minute totals for those eight seasons were, in order, 144, 146, 125, 167, 124, 92, 85, and 87. He scored just 42 goals in 12 seasons in the league. Horner retired after the 1939-40 season and was appointed the Maple Leafs' "goodwill ambassador."

## GORDIE HOWE

THE ONLY PLAYER to be named a first- or second-team NHL All-Star more than 15 times.

The amazing career of Gordie Howe lasted from his debut in 1946 with the Detroit Red Wings and ended at the age of 52 with the Hartford Whalers in 1980. He was a first-team or second-team NHL All-Star an unprecedented 21 times, placing first 12 seasons and second nine times. Counting his 6 seasons in the WHA, Howe played 32 seasons, appeared in 2,186 games, scored 975 goals, had 1,383 assists, and scored 2,358 points.

## MARK AND MARTY HOWE

THE ONLY TWO players to play on the same NHL team with their father.

Mark and Marty Howe were the only NHL players to play on the same team as their father, the immortal Gordie Howe, with the Hartford Whalers in 1979-80. The three also played together for six seasons in the World Hockey Association with the Houston Aeros from 1973 to 1977 and with the New England Whalers from 1977 to 1979.

## Harry Howell

THE ONLY PLAYER to appear in over 1,400 regular-season games without ever playing on a Stanley Cup champion.

Harry Howell holds not only the record for the longest career without playing on a Stanley Cup champion, but also the records for the most games without an appearance in a Stanley Cup final and the most games without playing on a first-place team. His 1,411 regular-season games are the fifth most in NHL history. He was with the New York Rangers (1952-53 to 1968-69), the Oakland and California Seals (1969-70 and 1970-71), and the Los Angeles Kings (1970-71 to 1972-73).

## BOBBY HULL

THE ONLY LEFT wing to score 610 career NHL goals.

Bobby Hull holds the record for most career goals by a left wing with 610 in the NHL and 303 in the WHA with his speed on the ice and his lightning-quick slap shots. He debuted with the Chicago Blackhawks in 1957-58 and stayed through 1971-72. Hull bolted the NHL for a lucrative contract with the Winnipeg Jets of the WHA in 1972-73, and stayed with the Jets throughout the seven-year existence of the league. When the WHA folded and the Jets were one of four teams admitted into the NHL, Hull played his final season, 1979-80, back in the NHL.

## Brett Hull

THE ONLY RIGHT wing to score more than 80 goals in a season.

Bobby Hull's son Brett set the all-time record for goals by a right wing in a season with 72 for the St. Louis Blues in 1989-90, then shattered the mark with 86 in 1990-91. Only Wayne Gretzky, with 92 in 1981-82 and 87 in 1983-84, has scored more goals in a season.

## PUNCH IMLACH

THE ONLY COACH to win the Stanley Cup with players of an average age of 31.

Punch Imlach's 1966-67 Toronto Maple Leafs, with an average age of 31, is the oldest team in NHL history to win the Stanley Cup. Toronto finished third in the six-team league with a record of 32-27-11, but in the playoffs defeated the first-place Chicago Blackhawks and the second-place Montreal Canadiens, both in six-game series. Standout players included Red Kelly (age 39), Terry Sawchuck (37), Tim Horton (37), Allan Stanley (41), Marcel Pronovost (36), Frank Mahovlich (29), and Dave Keon (27).

## Dick Irvin

THE ONLY COACH to lose 12 Stanley Cup finals.

Dick Irvin coached in 16 Stanley Cup finals, but managed to win only 4. The winners were with the Toronto Maple Leafs in 1932 and the Montreal Canadiens in 1944, 1946, and 1953. Irvin was on the losing end with the Chicago Blackhawks in 1931, with Toronto in 1933, 1935, 1936, 1938, 1939, and 1940, and with Montreal in 1947, 1951, 1952, 1954, and 1955.

## Doug Jarvis

THE ONLY PLAYER to appear in more than 920 consecutive games.

Doug Jarvis played in an NHL record 964 consecutive games from October 8, 1975, through October 10, 1987. The streak represented his entire career, in which he did not miss a single game. It ended only because he was released by the Hartford Whalers two games into the 1987-88 season. Jarvis played for the Montreal Canadiens from 1975-76 through 1981-82, for the Washington Capitals from 1982-83 through 1985-86, and for Hartford the remainder of his career.

## Bob Johnson

THE ONLY COACH to win the Stanley Cup after losing the first game of all four play-off series.

The 1990-91 Pittsburgh Penguins under coach Bob Johnson defied the odds to win the Stanley Cup. Entering the play-offs with the eighth best regular-season record in the NHL, the Penguins lost the first game of all four play-off series by an aggregate score of 18-10, but came back to beat the New Jersey Devils in seven games, the Washington Capitals in five games, the Boston Bruins in six contests, and the Minnesota North Stars in a six-game final.

## Doug Keans

THE ONLY GOALTENDER to allow two goals in the first 24 seconds of a game.

Doug Keans of the Los Angeles Kings had a nightmare of a game against the Edmonton Oilers on March 28, 1982, in Los Angeles. He allowed a goal to Mark Messier after 14 seconds of play and another to Dave Lumley 10 seconds later, and the Kings were quickly in a 2-0 hole. Keans was removed at 10:51 of the first period with Los Angeles losing 4-0. He was replaced by Mike Blake, who was making his NHL debut, and the Oilers went on to win 6-2.

# RED KELLY

THE ONLY PLAYER to win four Stanley Cups on two different teams.

Red Kelly played on eight Stanley Cup champions, four each with the Detroit Red Wings and the Toronto Maple Leafs. He was with Detroit's championship teams in 1949-50, 1951-52, 1953-54, and 1954-55. Kelly was on Toronto's title clubs in 1961-62, 1962-63, 1963-64, and 1966-67.

## George Kennedy

THE ONLY COACH whose team scored 16 goals in one game.

George Kennedy's Montreal Canadiens set the all-time NHL record for most goals scored in one game with a 16-3 thrashing of the Quebec Bulldogs on March 3, 1920, at Quebec.

## DAVE KEON

THE ONLY PLAYER to score two shorthand goals in one game in a Stanley Cup final.

Dave Keon shined for the Toronto Maple Leafs in the Cup-clinching game against the Detroit Red Wings on April 18, 1963. He scored two shorthand goals in the Toronto 3-1 win, which gave the Maple Leafs a four-games-to-one series victory.

## TIM KERR

THE ONLY PLAYER to score more than 32 power-play goals in a season.

Tim Kerr blasted home 58 goals for the Philadelphia Flyers in 1985-86, a record 34 of them on the power play. Kerr also holds the record for most power-play goals in one period in the play-offs, with three on April 13, 1985, in the second period of a 6-5 Philadelphia win over the Rangers in New York. Kerr scored four goals overall in the period in just 8:16 as the Flyers erased a 3-2 deficit.

## PETR KLIMA

THE ONLY PLAYER to score a goal in a Stanley Cup final game after more than 55 minutes of overtime.

Petr Klima of the Edmonton Oilers scored the goal that ended the longest Stanley Cup final game in history. It came on May 15, 1990, after 55:13 of overtime and gave the Oilers a 3-2 win over the Bruins at Boston Garden. The Bruins trailed 2-0 entering the third period, but Ray Bourque sent the game into overtime with goals at 3:43 and 18:31. After a 25-minute delay due to faulty lighting, Klima's shot through the pads of Boston goaltender Andy Moog ended the festivities.

## CHRIS KONTOS

THE ONLY PLAYER with six power-play goals in one play-off series.

Chris Kontos was not counted to provide much in the way of goal scoring for the Los Angeles Kings in their play-off series against the Edmonton Oilers in 1989. He had only two goals all year and only twenty-five in a seven-year NHL career. But Kontos stunned everyone with six power-play goals in the series as the Kings won in seven games. In the 1989-90 season, Kontos returned to his old ways and scored only two goals before being shipped to New Haven in the American Hockey League.

## Don Kozak

THE ONLY PLAYER to score after just six seconds of play in a Stanley Cup match.

Don Kozak scored the quickest goal in Stanley Cup history on April 17, 1977, by scoring just six seconds after face-off for the Kings against the Boston Bruins in Los Angeles. The Kings went on to win 7-4.

## JARI KURRI

THE ONLY PLAYER to score 12 goals in a Stanley Cup series.

Jari Kurri scored 12 goals for the Edmonton Oilers against the Chicago Blackhawks in the 1985 Campbell Conference final. Edmonton set a team record for most goals in one series with 44 in winning the best-of-seven series 4-2. Kurri and Wayne Gretzky were an unbeatable duo for the Stanley Cup champion Oilers in 1984-85. Kurri scored 71 goals, Gretzky 73, becoming the only pair of teammates who each scored at least 60 goals in a season.

## Andre Lacroix

THE ONLY PLAYER to score over 750 points in the World Hockey Association.

Andre Lacroix was the leading scorer in the seven-year existence of the World Hockey Association, which lasted from 1972-73 through 1978-79. Lacroix had 251 goals and 547 assists for 798 points during those seven seasons while playing for the Philadelphia Blazers, New York Golden Blades, New Jersey Knights, San Diego Mariners, Houston Aeros, and New England Whalers.

## PAT LAFONTAINE

THE ONLY PLAYER to score a goal in the fourth overtime of the seventh game of a play-off series.

The play-off match between the New York Islanders and the Capitals in Washington on April 18, 1987, is the fifth longest in NHL history, the longest since 1943, and the longest seventh game of all time. It ended at 1:55 a.m. on Easter Sunday after 68:47 of overtime when Pat LaFontaine of the Islanders smacked a rising shot into the net from just inside the blue line. It gave the Islanders a 3-2 win and a victory in the divisional semifinal series after trailing three games to one.

## Reggie Leach

THE ONLY PLAYER to score a goal in nine consecutive play-off games.

Reggie Leach scored 14 goals in nine consecutive games for the Philadelphia Flyers during the Stanley Cup play-offs in 1976. The streak began on April 17 in Toronto against the Maple Leafs, extended through the series against the Boston Bruins, and ended in the first game of the finals on May 9 versus the Canadiens in Montreal. During the streak, Leach had a five-goal game on May 6 in a 6-3 win over the Bruins in Philadelphia.

## Mikko Leinonen

THE ONLY ROOKIE with six assists in a play-off game.

The New York Rangers received a stellar performance from an unexpected source in a play-off game against the Philadelphia Flyers at Madison Square Garden in a 7-3 win on April 8, 1982. Mikko Leinonen became the only rookie, and the only player other than Wayne Gretzky, to be credited with six assists in a play-off game. Leinonen's feeds went to six different goal scorers. During the 1981-82 season, Leinonen had only 20 assists in 53 games. He had just 78 in 162 career games and only 5 in the 19 other play-off games he appeared in in the NHL.

## MARIO LEMIEUX

THE ONLY PLAYER to score a goal in every possible situation in one game.

Mario Lemieux put on perhaps the greatest one-game, one-man performance in NHL history for the Penguins on December 31, 1988, against the New Jersey Devils in Pittsburgh. Lemieux had five goals and three assists in Pittsburgh's 8-6 triumph. He scored a goal while the teams were at even strength, one on a power play, one while the Penguins were short-handed, and once on a penalty shot. Lemieux sent the festive New Year's Eve crowd home in a frenzy with a goal into an empty net.

## Tony Leswick

THE ONLY PLAYER to score a goal off the gloved hand of an opponent in overtime of the seventh game of a Stanley Cup final.

The bitter, hard-fought 1954 Stanley Cup final between the Detroit Red Wings and the Montreal Canadiens came to an abrupt conclusion in game seven on April 16 in Detroit. Tony Leswick scored the winner for the Red Wings at 4:29 of overtime to break a 1-1 tie after he took a pass from Glen Skov and shot from 40 feet. Montreal defenseman Doug Harvey tried to swat the shot out of the air with his gloved hand, but instead deflected the puck over the shoulder of goaltender Gerry McNeil.

## Ken Linseman and Doug Gilmour

THE ONLY TWO players to score goals two seconds apart in an NHL game.

With 10 seconds remaining in the game between the St. Louis Blues and the Bruins in Boston on December 19, 1987, Ken Linseman of the Bruins scored to cut the St. Louis lead to 6-5. Boston pulled goalie Doug Keans for an extra attacker before the face-off. Two seconds after Linseman's goal, Doug Gilmour of the Blues shot a goal into an empty net to give St. Louis a 7-5 win.

## Howard Lockhart

THE ONLY PLAYER to give up three five-goal games to opposing players in a six-week period.

Hamilton Tigers goaltender Howard Lockhart must have felt shell-shocked after allowing three players in six weeks to score at least five goals in a game. On January 26, 1921, Corb Denneny of the Toronto St. Patricks scored six times against Lockhart in a 10-3 win in Toronto. Newsy Lalonde of the Canadiens scored five on February 16 to beat Lockhart and Hamilton 10-5 in Montreal. Then Corb's brother Cy Denneny had six goals for the Ottawa Senators in a 12-5 win over Hamilton on March 7.

## Sam LoPresti

THE ONLY GOALTENDER to stop 80 shots in a regular-season game.

The good news was that Chicago Blackhawks goalie Sam LoPresti stopped an NHL regular-season record 80 shots against the Bruins on March 4, 1941, at the Boston Garden. The bad news was that he let three goals past him, and Chicago lost 3-2. Eddie Wiseman of Boston broke the 2-2 tie with a goal at 17:29 of the third period.

## Los Angeles Kings

THE ONLY TEAM to win a game in which 85 penalties were called.

The Los Angeles Kings and the Edmonton Oilers combined for 85 penalties on February 28, 1990, in Los Angeles. Edmonton had 44, the most ever by one team, receiving 26 minors, seven majors, six 10-minute misconducts, four game misconducts, and one match penalty. The Kings had 41 penalties. The fighting got so out of hand that the officials sent the teams to the locker rooms with 3:22 remaining in the second period for a cooling-off period. Somehow, in the midst of the fights, a hockey game was played, and the Kings won 4-2.

## Al MacInnis

THE ONLY DEFENSEMAN to lead the Stanley Cup play-offs in scoring.

Al MacInnis of the Calgary Flames became the only defenseman in NHL history to lead the Stanley Cup play-offs in scoring with seven goals and 24 assists for 31 points in 1989. The effort by MacInnis helped Calgary win the Stanley Cup, which culminated in a six-game final series win over the Montreal Canadiens.

## CONNIE MADIGAN

THE ONLY PLAYER to make his NHL debut at the age of 38.

Connie Madigan is the oldest player ever to make his NHL debut. He was 38 years, four months, and two days old when he played in his first game as a defenseman with the St. Louis Blues on February 6, 1973, in a 5-1 win over the Vancouver Canucks in St. Louis. Madigan's NHL career lasted only 20 games with no goals and three assists.

## Joe Malone

THE ONLY PLAYER to score seven goals in an NHL game.

Joe Malone is the only player in NHL history to score seven goals in a game and the only one to score at least six goals in a game twice in his career. The seven-goal game was on January 31, 1920, as Malone led his Quebec Bulldogs to a 10-6 win over the Toronto St. Patricks in Quebec. Malone scored six on March 10, 1920, in a 10-4 triumph over Ottawa at Quebec. During the 1917-18 season, Malone had 44 goals in 20 games and added 39 more in 24 contests in 1919-20.

## JACK MARSHALL

THE ONLY SKATER to play on four different Stanley Cup champions.

Jack Marshall became the only skater to play on four different Stanley Cup champions as a member of the Winnipeg Victorias in 1901, the Montreal AAA in 1902, the Montreal Wanderers in 1907 and 1910, and the Toronto Blueshirts in 1914.

## Bill Masterton

THE ONLY PLAYER to die from injuries suffered in an NHL game.

In a 2-2 tie against the Oakland Seals in Bloomington, Minnesota, on January 13, 1968, North Stars center Bill Masterton was checked cleanly into the boards, lost his balance, and hit his head heavily on the ice surface. He died a little more than 24 hours later from massive brain damage in a hospital in the Minneapolis suburb of Edina. Masterton is the only fatality in NHL history.

## MARKUS MATTSSON

THE ONLY GOALTENDER to stop an opposing player's 51-game scoring streak.

Markus Mattsson was near the end of an undistinguished career when he stood in goal for the Los Angeles Kings on January 28, 1984, against Wayne Gretzky and the Edmonton Oilers in Los Angeles. Gretzky had scored a goal or an assist in an NHL-record 51 consecutive games entering the contest, but was shut out by Mattsson as the Kings won 4-2. Gretzky's final chance came with a shot with two seconds remaining, but Mattsson smothered the puck. Gretzky had 61 goals and 92 assists during the 51-game scoring streak.

## KEN MCAULEY

THE ONLY GOALTENDER to allow four goals in one minute and 20 seconds.

Ken McAuley had a difficult time backstopping a couple of horrible New York Rangers teams in 1943-44 and 1944-45. He had a goals-against average of 5.61 and a won-lost-tied record of 17-64-15. On January 21, 1945, against the Bruins in Boston, McAuley allowed four goals in one minute and 20 seconds of the second period in a 14-3 loss. Bill Thoms scored at 6:34 of the period, Frank Mario at 7:08 and 7:27, and Ken Smith at 7:54. Mario scored only nine goals in his entire NHL career.

## LANNY MCDONALD

THE ONLY PLAYER to score four goals in a losing cause in a play-off game.

Lanny McDonald scored four goals for the Toronto Maple Leafs on April 17, 1977, against the Philadelphia Flyers in Toronto, but the Flyers won 6-5 in overtime. McDonald's fourth goal, at 12:44 of the third period, gave the Maple Leafs a 5-2 lead, but his teammates could not hold the three-goal advantage.

## FRANK MCGEE

THE ONLY PLAYER to score 14 goals in a Stanley Cup match.

Despite the handicap of being blind in one eye, Frank McGee of the Ottawa Silver Seven scored an incredible 14 goals in a Stanley Cup game on January 16, 1905, in a 23-2 pasting of the Dawson City Klondikers. McGee scored eight goals in a span of eight minutes and 20 seconds during the second half.

## Doug McKay

THE ONLY PLAYER whose lone NHL game was on a Stanley Cup champion in the finals.

Doug McKay's only NHL game was as a member of the Stanley Cup champion Detroit Red Wings in the 1950 finals against the New York Rangers. His brief NHL career lasted only a few minutes.

## Johnny McKinnon and Hap Day

THE ONLY TWO defensemen to score four goals in the same game.

A defenseman scoring at least four goals in a game has happened only nine times by seven different players in NHL history, but Johnny McKinnon of the Pittsburgh Pirates and Hap Day of the Toronto Maple Leafs both scored four goals on November 19, 1929, in a 10-5 Pirate win in Pittsburgh. McKinnon scored only ten goals during the entire 1929-30 season, and Day had only seven. It would be 48 years before another NHL defenseman scored four goals in a game.

## MAJOR FRED MCLAUGHLIN

THE ONLY OWNER to hire a stranger he met on a train to coach his team.

Eccentric Major Fred McLaughlin founded the Chicago Blackhawks in 1926 and made 11 coaching changes in the first nine years of the team's existence. The most bizarre hiring was that of Godfrey Matheson in 1932. McLaughlin met Matheson on a train between Minneapolis and Chicago and was so impressed by Matheson's knowledge of hockey that he was appointed as the Chicago head coach. Mathseon was fired by midseason.

## Gilles Meloche

THE ONLY GOALTENDER to allow over 2,700 goals in a career.

Gilles Meloche was saddled with backstopping horrible teams during much of his NHL career with the Chicago Blackhawks, California Seals, Cleveland Barons, Minnesota North Stars, and Pittsburgh Penguins from 1970 through 1988. He allowed a league record 2,756 goals in 788 games. He had a career won-lost-tied record of 270-351-131.

## Stan Mikita

THE ONLY PLAYER to win the Art Ross, Hart Memorial, and Lady Byng trophies in the same season.

Stan Mikita won the Art Ross Trophy as the NHL's leading scorer; the Hart Memorial Trophy, awarded to the Most Valuable Player; and the Lady Byng Trophy, given to the player who best combines sportsmanship with a high standard of play, in both 1966-67 and 1967-68 while playing for the Chicago Blackhawks. No other player has ever won all three awards in the same season, even once. In the two seasons he swept the three awards, Mikita scored 184 points with only 26 minutes in penalties.

## MINNESOTA NORTH STARS

THE ONLY TEAM to lose a game in which 406 penalty minutes were assessed.

The Minnesota North Stars lost a game and a fight to the Bruins on February 26, 1981, in Boston. The final score was 5-1, and a record 406 minutes in penalties were assessed to the combatants, 211 of which went to the North Stars. A huge fight at the end of the first period spilled over into the Boston Garden runway and resulted in 12 players being ejected. The two teams combined for 38 minors, 26 majors, seven 10-minute misconducts, and 13 game misconducts.

## Ivan Mitchell

THE ONLY GOALTENDER to allow an opposing player at least six goals twice in a month.

There have been only eight occurrences in NHL history in which a player has scored at least six goals in a game, but Mitchell managed to be victimized twice in a month. Playing for the Toronto St. Pats, Mitchell gave up six goals to Newsy Lalonde of the Montreal Canadiens on January 10, 1920, in a 14-7 loss. On January 31, Mitchell gave up an NHL record seven goals to Joe Malone of the Quebec Bulldogs as Toronto lost 10-6. Mitchell's NHL career lasted only 21 games.

## MONTREAL

THE ONLY CITY to be represented by six different Stanley Cup champion teams.

Six different teams representing the city of Montreal have captured the Stanley Cup. The Montreal Victorias won four in a row beginning in 1895-96. The Montreal Shamrocks claimed the Cup in both 1898-99 and 1899-1900. Montreal AAA won in 1901-02 and 1902-03. The Montreal Wanderers were next with four championships between 1905-06 and 1909-10. The fabled Montreal Canadiens won the first of their 24 trophies in 1915-16. And the Montreal Maroons won in 1925-26 and 1934-35.

## BILL MOSIENKO

THE ONLY PLAYER to score three goals in 21 seconds.

Bill Mosienko of the Chicago Blackhawks scored the quickest hat trick in NHL history on March 23, 1952, against the Rangers in New York. With Chicago trailing 6-2 and the two teams at even strength, Mosienko scored at 6:09, 6:20, and 6:30 of the third period and keyed a comeback which resulted in a 7-6 Chicago win. Gus Bodnar assisted on all three goals. Mosienko narrowly missed a fourth goal seconds later when a shot hit the post. The Ranger goaltender was Lorne Anderson, who was playing in his third, and last, NHL game.

## PETE MULDOON

THE ONLY COACH to have a fictitious curse named after him.

Pete Muldoon was the first coach of the Chicago Blackhawks in 1926-27 and was fired after one season. In 1941, Toronto sportswriter James X. Coleman was stuck for a story and said the reason that Chicago had never finished first was because Muldoon had put a curse on the team when he was relieved of his coaching duties. "The Curse of the Muldoon" was pure fiction but was accepted as fact and gained momentum through the years as the Blackhawks failed to finish first until 1966-67, the 41st year of the franchise.

## Grant Mulvey

THE ONLY PLAYER to score four goals in the first period of an NHL game.

Grant Mulvey of the Chicago Blackhawks scored four goals in the first period of a game against the St. Louis Blues on February 3, 1982, in Chicago Stadium. The quick start, and another Mulvey goal in the third period along with two assists, enabled the Blackhawks to win 9-5. Mulvey is also the only right wing to score four goals in any period. Ironically, Grant's scoring outburst came only a few days after the Los Angeles Kings released his brother Paul, which ended Paul's four-year NHL career.

## MIKE MURPHY

THE ONLY COACH whose club surrendered 13 goals in a Stanley Cup game.

Mike Murphy's Los Angeles Kings allowed a record 13 goals to the high-powered Edmonton Oilers in a Stanley Cup match on April 9, 1987, in Edmonton. The Oilers won 13-3 as Jari Kurri had four goals and Wayne Gretzky had a goal and a play-off record-tying six assists. The Oilers went on to win the series four games to one.

## BRYAN MURRAY

THE ONLY COACH to be fired and replaced by his brother.

Bryan Murray was in his ninth season as coach of the Washington Capitals when he was fired on January 15, 1990, with an 18-24-4 record. The Capitals kept the coaching job in the Murray family, however, by hiring Bryan's younger brother Terry, who had been coach of the Baltimore Skipjacks, Washington's farm team in the American Hockey League. Under Terry Murray, the Capitals were 18-14-2 for the remainder of the 1989-90 season. Bryan Murray was named coach of the Detroit Red Wings before the start of the 1990-91 season.

## Mats Naslund

THE ONLY PLAYER with five assists in an All-Star Game.

Mats Naslund of the Montreal Canadiens starred in the All-Star Game on February 9, 1988, in St. Louis with a record five assists in leading the Wales Conference to a 6-5 win.

## New York Americans

THE ONLY NHL team owned by a convicted bootlegger.

The New York Americans were in the NHL from 1925 through 1941, and are known for three things. They were the first team from New York in the league, predating the Rangers by one year; they had stars all over their uniforms; and they were owned by convicted bootlegger William Dwyer. Dwyer was the head of one of the greatest rum-running syndicates of the Prohibition era and enjoyed a reputation as the "king of the bootleggers." While he owned the Americans, he spent 13 months in the Atlanta federal penitentiary for his criminal activities.

## New York Rangers

THE ONLY TEAM to go without a Stanley Cup championship for more than 50 years.

New York Rangers fans have long suffered through the frustration of Stanley Cup failures. The last Stanley Cup championship was in 1940, when the Rangers defeated the Toronto Maple Leafs four games to two. The Rangers also hold the record for the longest period between first-place finishes, which is 48 years. After ending the regular season in first place in 1941-42, the Rangers did not finish first again until 1989-90.

## CHRIS NILAN

THE ONLY PLAYER with 10 penalties in one game.

Chris Nilan of the Boston Bruins had an NHL record 10 penalties on March 31, 1991, in a 7-3 win over the Hartford Whalers at the Boston Garden. He had six minors, two majors, one 10-minute misconduct, and one game misconduct. Among Nilan's infractions were holding, fighting, roughing, elbowing, and unsportsmanlike conduct.

## Adam Oates

THE ONLY PLAYER with four assists in one period in an All-Star Game.

Boston Bruins standout Adam Oates dished out four assists in the first 13:22 of the All-Star Game on February 6, 1993, in Montreal. The last of Oates's four assists gave the Wales Conference a 6-0 lead and set the pace for a 16-6 rout.

## WILLIE O'REE

THE ONLY BLACK player in the NHL during the 1957-58 season.

Willie O'Ree became the first black player in NHL history on January 18, 1958, when he debuted with the Boston Bruins in a 3-0 win over the Canadiens in Montreal. A native of Fredericton, New Brunswick, O'Ree played in just 45 NHL games.

## TERRY O'REILLY

THE ONLY COACH to lose a Stanley Cup final in which a game was stopped in the second period by a power outage.

Terry O'Reilly's Boston Bruins were trailing the Edmonton Oilers three games to none in the 1988 Stanley Cup final when they took the ice on May 24 at Boston Garden. The Oilers had just tied the score 3-3 at 16:37 of the second period when the arena went dark due to a power shortage. The game was stopped and declared a shortened 3-3 tie. It was decided to replay the game in Boston as game seven only if necessary. The Oilers took the Stanley Cup with a 6-3 win on May 26 at Edmonton.

## Bobby Orr

THE ONLY DEFENSEMAN to win a scoring title.

Bobby Orr revolutionized the role of a defenseman during his years in the NHL from 1966 through 1979 by becoming an offensive force with his play-making and goal-scoring capabilities. Orr won the NHL scoring title with the Boston Bruins in 1969-70 and 1974-75 and was runner-up in the scoring race three times. His 102 assists in 1970-71 is a record for a defenseman. The only other two players with over 100 assists in a season are Wayne Gretzky and Mario Lemieux. Orr won eight consecutive James Norris Trophies from 1967-68 through 1974-75.

## OTTAWA SENATORS

THE ONLY TEAM to lose 38 road games in a row.

The Ottawa Senators, a first-year expansion team, lost their first 38 road games in 1992-93 to set an NHL record. The streak finally ended on April 10, 1993, with a win over the New York Islanders in the Nassau Veterans' Memorial Coliseum. Ottawa won 5-3 when Laurie Boschman scored two goals in the final minute to complete a hat trick.

## Ottawa Silver Seven

THE ONLY TEAM to kick the Stanley Cup trophy into a canal.

The Stanley Cup trophy has suffered numerous indignities over the years. It was once left in a photographer's studio and was used to plant geraniums. It was left by the side of the road in 1924 while the Montreal Canadiens changed a flat tire. And it was stolen twice by disgruntled fans. The Ottawa Silver Seven, who won the trophy four years in a row beginning in 1903, kicked the Cup onto the frozen Rideau Canal in a night of drunken revelry. The team rushed back the next morning to find the Cup resting on top of the ice.

## Mike Palmateer and Tony Esposito

THE ONLY TWO goaltenders to allow five goals in 84 seconds.

Mike Palmateer of the Toronto Maple Leafs and Tony Esposito of the Chicago Blackhawks allowed the five fastest goals in NHL history on October 15, 1983, in Toronto. In the second period Gaston Gingras of Toronto scored at 16:49, Denis Savard of Chicago at 17:12, Steve Larmer of the Blackhawks at 17:27, Savard again at 17:42, and John Anderson of the Maple Leafs at 18:13. Toronto won the contest 10-8.

## BERNIE PARENT

THE ONLY GOALTENDER to have to be taken out of a play-off game because an opposing player threw his mask into the stands.

With the Toronto Maple Leafs leading the New York Rangers 4-1 with 4:42 left in regulation at Madison Square Garden in game two of their play-off series on April 8, 1971, Vic Hadfield of the Rangers and Jim Harrison of the Maple Leafs faced off in a good, old-fashioned fight. Toronto goaltender Bernie Parent leaped in to defend Harrison, and Hadfield ripped off Parent's mask and threw it into the stands. Parent had no spare, and had to be taken out of the game.

## PETE PEETERS

THE ONLY GOALTENDER to put together two undefeated streaks of 25 or more games in a career.

Pete Peeters owns the second and third longest undefeated streaks by a goaltender in NHL history. In 1979-80 with the Philadelphia Flyers, he was unbeaten in 27 consecutive games with 22 wins and five ties. In 1982-83, as a member of the Boston Bruins, he had an undefeated streak of 31 in a row, one short of Gerry Cheevers's record, during which he won 26 and tied five.

## Don Perry

THE ONLY COACH whose team gave up eight goals in a Stanley Cup play-off game, and won.

Don Perry's Los Angeles Kings surrendered eight goals to the Edmonton Oilers in the first game of the Stanley Cup series on April 7, 1982, in Edmonton, but the Kings still won 10-8. The Oilers led 4-1 after the first 9:02 of play, but Los Angeles fought back. Since the Oilers were 48-17-15 in regular-season play and the Kings had a record of 24-41-15, Edmonton entered the series as huge favorites. But the first-game upset set the stage for Los Angeles to win the series three games to two.

## PHILADELPHIA BLAZERS

THE ONLY MAJOR league hockey team to have its first home game postponed because the ice was deemed unsafe.

The Philadelphia Blazers of the World Hockey Association should have known what was in store for them when they scheduled the first home game in franchise history for Friday the 13th, 1972, against the New England Whalers. At game time the ice was choppy and cracking, and the resurfacing machine meant to repair the problem fell through the ice. Blazer president Jim Cooper drew boos and a hail of souvenir pucks from fans when he announced the postponement of the game.

## Randy Pierce

THE ONLY PLAYER assessed a penalty for kissing a puck.

Randy Pierce of the Colorado Rockies was so thrilled with an insurance goal scored at 19:27 of the third period in a 7-4 win over the Islanders in Denver on November 28, 1979, that he kissed the puck and tossed it into the stands. Pierce was given a two-minute penalty for delay of game. It was the first time the Rockies had ever defeated the Islanders.

## Pittsburgh Penguins

THE ONLY TEAM to win 17 straight regular-season games.

The 1992-93 Pittsburgh Penguins set NHL records for most consecutive regular-season wins, but failed in its attempt to win a third straight Stanley Cup. The Penguins' 17-game regular-season streak broke the previous record of 15, set by the 1981-82 New York Islanders. The record breaker came on April 9, when Mario Lemieux scored five goals in a 10-4 win over the Rangers in New York. The streak ended in a 6-6 tie against the Devils in New Jersey on April 14. Pittsburgh lost a second-round play-off series to the Islanders in seven games.

## Jacques Plante

THE ONLY GOALTENDER to lead the NHL in goals-against average seven times.

Jacques Plante was superb in goal for the Montreal Canadiens, leading the league in goals-against average seven times, in 1955-56, 1956-57, 1957-58, 1958-59, 1959-60, 1961-62, and 1962-63. He was the Montreal goalie during their streak of five consecutive Stanley Cup titles between 1955-56 and 1959-60. Plante is best known, however, as the goaltender who pioneered the use of the facemask. He was the first to use the protection on a regular basis, beginning in 1959.

## DENIS POTVIN

THE ONLY DEFENSEMAN to score three goals with two assists in a play-off game.

All-Star Denis Potvin became the only defenseman with three goals and two assists in a play-off game in leading the New York Islanders to a 6-3 win over the Edmonton Oilers on April 17, 1981, on Long Island. Potvin's third goal broke a 3-3 tie at 3:47 of the third period.

## Joe Primeau

THE ONLY COACH to win a Stanley Cup final in which every game was settled in overtime.

Joe Primeau's Toronto Maple Leafs won the 1951 Stanley Cup final against the Montreal Canadiens in a series in which all five games were decided in overtime. Toronto won the first game 3-2 and Montreal the second, also 3-2, before the Maple Leafs won three in a row, 2-1, 3-2, and 3-2, capturing the final on home ice. Oddly, all of the overtimes were relatively short. The longest was the first game, which ended at 5:51 of OT on a goal by Sid Smith. The shortest overtime of the series lasted 2:53.

## QUEBEC BULLDOGS

THE ONLY TEAM to allow more than seven goals per game in one season.

The Quebec Bulldogs franchise lasted only one year in the NHL, but it will probably be in the NHL record books forever because of a 7.4 goals-against average on 177 goals in 24 games in 1919-20. The Bulldogs finished the year with a 4-20-0 record.

## Quebec Nordiques

THE ONLY TEAM to improve their record by more than 40 points from one season to the next.

The Quebec Nordiques hit rock bottom in 1989-90, with a record of 12-61-7. The team improved slightly over the next two seasons and was 20-48-12 in 1991-92. The 1992-93 campaign was the great leap forward as the Nordiques went 47-27-10. The improvement from 52 points to 104 is easily the best in NHL history.

## Pat Quinn

THE ONLY COACH to go undefeated in 35 consecutive games.

The 1979-80 Philadelphia Flyers, under coach Pat Quinn, went undefeated in 35 consecutive games with 25 wins and 10 ties. The streak broke the record of 28 held by the 1977-78 Montreal Canadiens. The Flyers' streak started on October 14 and lasted until January 6, running the team's record on the season to 26-1-10. The end came on January 7 with a 7-1 loss to the North Stars in Minnesota. Philadelphia ended the regular season with a record 48-12-20. They reached the Stanley Cup finals, but lost to the New York Islanders.

## BILLY REAY

THE ONLY COACH whose club allowed seven goals in a Stanley Cup final, and won.

The game-five Stanley Cup final series matchup between Billy Reay's Chicago Blackhawks and the Canadiens in Montreal on May 8, 1973, was expected to be a low-scoring affair because the two teams possessed two of the best goaltenders of all time. But Ken Dryden of Montreal and Tony Esposito combined to allow 15 goals, the most ever in one game in a Stanley Cup final. There were eight goals scored in the second period. Chicago won 8-7, but lost game six and the Cup to Montreal 6-4.

## Jeff Reese

THE ONLY GOALTENDER with three assists in one game.

Jeff Reese of the Calgary Flames became the only goaltender to assist on three goals in one game in a 13-1 rout of the San Jose Sharks on February 10, 1993, in Calgary. Reese had one assist in each period, in helping to set up two goals by Robert Reichel and one by Gary Roberts. The Sharks scored the first goal of the game, and Calgary didn't tie it up until 12:26 of the first period, but then the rout was on.

## MR. AND MRS. LOU REESE

THE ONLY MARRIED couple to require stitches as the result of being hit in the face with separate pucks in an NHL game.

Mr. and Mrs. Lou Reese of Lansing, Michigan, attended a play-off game between the Red Wings and the Toronto Maple Leafs in Detroit on March 28, 1943. Early in the contest, a puck struck Mrs. Reese in the face, requiring four stitches, administered in the first-aid room. Just after she returned to her seat, another puck hit her husband in the nose. He needed two stitches. Mrs. Reese therefore beat her husband four stitches to two, which ironically was the final score as the Red Wings also won 4-2.

## EARL "DUTCH" REIBEL

THE ONLY PLAYER to assist on each of his team's four goals in his first NHL game.

Earl "Dutch" Reibel played in his first NHL game as a member of the Detroit Red Wings on October 8, 1953, and made an immediate splash with four assists in a 4-1 win over the New York Rangers in Detroit. Reibel assisted on goals by Red Kelly, Andre Pronovost, Gordie Howe, and Ted Lindsay. The only other player with four assists in his first game is Roland Eriksson of the Minnesota North Stars on October 6, 1976, in a 6-5 win over the New York Rangers at Madison Square Garden.

## Paul Reinhart

THE ONLY DEFENSEMAN with two hat tricks in the play-offs.

Paul Reinhart is the only defenseman with two hat tricks in play-off competition, and both times he did it while on the road playing for the Calgary Flames. The first came on April 14, 1983, at Edmonton against the Oilers, but the Flames lost 6-3. The second was on April 8, 1984, versus the Canucks in Vancouver in a 5-1 Calgary win.

## MANON RHÉAUME

THE ONLY WOMAN to play for an NHL team.

Manon Rhéaume played goaltender for the Tampa Bay Lightning in an exhibition game on September 23, 1992, in a 6-4 loss to the St. Louis Blues. She played one period, faced nine shots, and allowed two goals. Rhéaume was sent to the Atlanta Knights, a Tampa Bay farm team in the International Hockey League, where she played in two games. The second was a starting assignment on April 4, 1993, before 15,179 fans at the Omni. Rhéaume played the entire game in the 8-6 loss to the Cincinnati Cyclones.

## Henri Richard

THE ONLY INDIVIDUAL to play on 11 Stanley Cup champions.

Henri Richard played for the Montreal Canadiens from 1955-56 through 1974-75 and played on 11 Stanley Cup champions, more than any other player in NHL history. Jean Béliveau and Yvan Cournoyer each played on 10 Stanley Cup championship teams. Both, like Richard, played their entire career in a Montreal uniform.

## MAURICE RICHARD

THE ONLY PLAYER with six play-off overtime goals.

The first player to score 50 goals in a season (in a 50-game schedule, no less) and 500 goals in a career, Maurice Richard seemed to save the best of magnificent performances for the play-offs. With the Montreal Canadiens between 1942 and 1960, Richard scored six overtime goals in the play-offs, which still stands as the record. He had one in 1946, three in 1951, one in 1957, and one in 1958. Richard's best game may have been on March 23, 1944, when he scored all of Montreal's goals in a 5-1 win over the Toronto Maple Leafs at the Forum.

## Larry Robinson

THE ONLY PLAYER to appear in more than 220 play-off games.

All-Star defenseman Larry Robinson appeared in 227 play-off games during his 20-year NHL career. He was with the Montreal Canadiens from 1972-73 through 1988-89 and played for the Los Angeles Kings from 1989-90 until his retirement following the 1991-92 campaign. He appeared in the playoffs every year of his outstanding career.

## Luc Robitaille

THE ONLY LEFT wing to score more than 60 goals in a season.

Luc Robitaille set the NHL record for most goals scored and most points in a season by a left wing with the Los Angeles Kings in 1992-93. His 63 goals broke the record of 60 set by Steve Shutt with the Montreal Canadiens in 1976-77. Robitaille's 125 points bettered Kevin Stevens's mark of 123, which was established with the Pittsburgh Penguins in 1991-92.

## Al Rollins

THE ONLY GOALTENDER to win the Most Valuable Player trophy despite losing 47 games.

Chicago Blackhawks goaltender Al Rollins had a won-lost-tied record of 12-47-7 in 1953-54, the second most losses in NHL history, but still won the Hart Memorial Trophy given to the league's Most Valuable Player. Not only did the Blackhawks finish dead last that season, but the team surrendered 242 goals, 60 more than any other club in the league.

## Art Ross

THE ONLY COACH whose team compiled a season-winning percentage over .830.

The 1929-30 Boston Bruins under coach Art Ross compiled an .875 winning percentage, the highest in NHL history, with a 38-5-1 record. The Bruins did not fare so well in the Stanley Cup play-offs, however. The semifinal against the Montreal Maroons was a best-of-five affair, and the Bruins won three games to one, but the Montreal Canadiens were tougher in the best-of-three final. Montreal won 3-0 and 4-3 to take the Cup.

## CLAUDE RUEL

THE ONLY COACH with a season-winning percentage over .600 to miss the play-offs.

Claude Ruel's 1969-70 Montreal Canadiens had a record 38-22-16 for a winning percentage of .605, but missed the play-offs. The Canadiens finished in a fourth-place tie with the New York Rangers, who were also 38-22-16, but the Rangers made the play-offs on the basis of having scored 246 goals to Montreal's 244. On the final day of the season, the Rangers beat the Detroit Red Wings 9-5, and the Canadiens lost 10-2 to the Chicago Blackhawks to allow the Rangers to advance.

## San Jose Sharks

THE ONLY TEAM to lose more than 70 games in a season.

The San Jose Sharks and Ottawa Senators were neck and neck in the race to see which would become the losingest team in NHL history during the 1992-93 campaign. The old record was 67, set by the 1974-75 Washington Capitals. San Jose finished the year at 11-71-2, just nosing out Ottawa, which was 10-70-4. The Capitals' 1974-75 winning percentage of .131 remains the worst in NHL history.

## GLEN SATHER

THE ONLY COACH whose team scored at least 400 goals in a season.

Not only are Glen Sather's Edmonton Oilers the only team to score at least 400 goals in a season, but they did it five times in five consecutive seasons. Led by Wayne Gretzky, Mark Messier, Glenn Anderson, Jari Kurri, and Paul Coffey, the Oilers scored 417 goals in 1981-82, 424 in 1982-83, 446 in 1983-84, 401 in 1984-85, and 426 in 1985-86.

## TERRY SAWCHUCK

THE ONLY GOALTENDER to record more than 100 career shutouts.

Terry Sawchuck holds NHL records for most games by a goaltender (971), most wins (435), and most shutouts (103). He played from 1949-50 through 1969-70. Of his record shutouts, 85 were with the Detroit Red Wings, 11 with the Boston Bruins, 4 for the Toronto Maple Leafs, 2 with the Los Angeles Kings, and 1 in the final season of his career as a member of the New York Rangers. Sawchuck played on four Stanley Cup champions.

## Dave Schultz

THE ONLY PLAYER with at least 410 penalty minutes in one season.

The Stanley Cup champion Philadelphia Flyers of 1973-74 and 1974-75 were known as the "Broad Street Bullies" for their overly aggressive play. The team's number one enforcer was Dave Schultz, who in 1974-75 slashed, poked, checked, and fought his way to an NHL record 472 minutes in penalties.

## Al Secord

THE ONLY LEFT wing with four goals in one period.

Al Secord scored four goals in the second period for the Chicago Blackhawks from his position at left wing on January 7, 1987, in a 6-4 win over the Toronto Maple Leafs at Chicago Stadium. The Blackhawks entered the final period trailing 2-1 before Secord's heroics gave them the victory. Two of Secord's goals came 10 seconds apart.

## Teemu Selanne

THE ONLY ROOKIE with more than 70 goals in a season.

Teemu Selanne came from Finland to shatter the NHL goal-scoring record for rookies with the Winnipeg Jets in 1992-93. Selanne had 76 goals, which tied for the league lead and broke the previous rookie record of 53 by Mike Bossy of the New York Islanders in 1977-78.

## Fred Shero

THE ONLY COACH to win more than 35 home games in a season.

The 1975-76 Philadelphia Flyers, under coach Fred Shero, loved home cooking. They set a record for most wins during the regular season with a 36-2-2 mark at the Spectrum, including wins in the final 20 regular-season games and the first four in the play-offs. The Flyers were 15-11-14 on the road for a final record of 51-13-16. But in the Stanley Cup final, the Flyers were swept four straight by the Montreal Canadiens, which included two losses in Philadelphia.

## Risto Siltanen

THE ONLY DEFENSEMAN with five assists in a play-off game.

Risto Siltanen had only 29 assists for the Quebec Nordiques during the 1986-87 regular season, which would prove to be his last in the NHL. But on April 14, 1987, he became the only defenseman to accumulate five assists in a play-off game in a 7-5 win over the Whalers in Hartford. Siltanen also spread the puck around, as his five assists went to five different goal scorers.

## Darryl Sittler

THE ONLY PLAYER with more than eight points in one game.

Darryl Sittler had an amazing 10 points for the Toronto Maple Leafs on February 7, 1976, on six goals and four assists. No one else in NHL history has ever had more than eight points in one game. Sittler's onslaught came against the Boston Bruins in an 11-4 win at Maple Leaf Gardens. He had two assists in the first period, three goals and two assists in the second, and three goals in the third.

## Paul Skidmore

THE ONLY GOALTENDER to allow a goal in the first five seconds of his NHL career.

Goaltender Paul Skidmore received his first NHL start with the St. Louis Blues on December 20, 1981, against the Jets in Winnipeg and was initiated quickly. Five seconds after the opening face-off, Doug Smail scored for the Jets to set a league record (since tied by two others) for the fastest goal from the start of a game. Smail scored again in the third period to break a 3-3 tie, and the Jets won 5-4. Skidmore played only one other NHL game, a 6-1 win over the Colorado Rockies nine days later.

## BRIAN SKRUDLAND

THE ONLY PLAYER to score a Stanley Cup overtime goal after less than 10 seconds of play.

The Montreal Canadiens got help from some unexpected sources in game two of the Stanley Cup final against the Flames on May 18, 1986, in Calgary. In the overtime period, Brian Skrudland, a rookie who had scored only nine goals in the regular season, put the puck into the net after only eight seconds of play, the fastest overtime goal in Stanley Cup history. The 3-2 Montreal win tied the series at 1-1, and the Canadiens did not lose again, taking the series in five games.

## Alex Smart

THE ONLY PLAYER to score three goals in his first NHL game, and never score again.

Alex Smart breezed into the NHL on January 14, 1943, by scoring three goals in the first game of his career. Playing for the Montreal Canadiens, Smart scored twice in 14 seconds, at 19:40 and 19:54 of the second period, and added another in the third. He also had an assist in the Canadiens' 5-1 win over the Chicago Blackhawks in Montreal. Smart played in only seven more NHL games and never scored another goal.

## Billy Smith

THE ONLY GOALTENDER to be credited with a goal because an opposing player shot the puck into his own net.

In a game between the Colorado Rockies and the Islanders on November 28, 1979, in Denver, the Rockies pulled goaltender Bill McKenzie early in the third period for a sixth attacker. The plan backfired when Colorado's Rob Ramage sent a pass down the ice into the empty net. Since Islander goaltender Billy Smith was closest to the puck when Ramage shot the puck, Smith was credited with a goal. Ramage's mistake tied the score 4-4, but the Rockies recovered to win 7-4.

## GARY SMITH

THE ONLY GOALTENDER to be credited with 48 losses in a season.

Gary Smith suffered through a long year as goaltender of the California Seals in 1970-71 with a record of 19-48-4, the most losses by a goaltender in NHL history. The much-traveled Smith, nicknamed "Suitcase," played for the Toronto Maple Leafs, Chicago Blackhawks, Vancouver Canucks, Minnesota North Stars, Washington Capitals, and Winnipeg Jets during his career, with a final record of 152-237-67 between 1965 and 1980.

## Sid Smith

THE ONLY PLAYER to score three power-play goals in one game in a Stanley Cup final.

Sid Smith put a charge in the Toronto Maple Leaf power play on April 10, 1949, by setting a Stanley Cup finals record with three power-play goals against the Red Wings in Detroit to account for all of his team's scores in a 3-1 win. Smith scored twice in a 66-second span in the first period and once more in the second. The victory came in the second game of a four-game series sweep.

## STEVE SMITH

THE ONLY PLAYER to knock a game-winning goal into his team's own net in game seven of a Stanley Cup series.

In game seven of the series between the Edmonton Oilers and Calgary Flames on April 30, 1986, the score was tied 2-2 five minutes into the third period when Oiler defenseman Steve Smith's clearing pass struck the skate of goaltender Grant Fuhr and caromed into the net. The goal was credited to Perry Berezan, but he wasn't within 10 feet of the puck. There was no more scoring as Calgary won 3-2. Not only did Smith wear the goat horns, but it happened on his 23rd birthday.

## CONN SMYTHE

THE ONLY OWNER to obtain a future Hall of Fame player by betting on a horse.

The Toronto Maple Leafs had a chance to purchase star defenseman King Clancy from the Ottawa Senators in 1930 for $35,000, but team owner Conn Smythe didn't have that much cash on hand. He borrowed part of the money from friends, then bet it on a long-shot horse. The horse won, and Smythe had the purchase price for Clancy. While with the Maple Leafs, Clancy was a first- or second-team All-Star four times.

## Vic Stasiuk

THE ONLY COACH whose club was tied 24 times in a season.

Vic Stasiuk's Philadelphia Flyers set the NHL record for most ties in a season in 1969-70 when they were deadlocked 24 times. But when the Flyers most needed a tie, they couldn't come up with one. Philadelphia needed just one point in the last six games to reach the play-offs, but lost all six including a 1-0 loss in the finale to the Minnesota North Stars on a shot from center ice. The Flyers finished 17-35-24. The Flyers were knocked out of the play-offs because they had fewer wins than the Oakland Seals.

## Anton and Peter Stastny

THE ONLY TWO players with eight points in a road game.

The only two players to accumulate eight points in a road game are brothers who accomplished the feat in the same game. They are also the only two rookies with eight points in a game. It happened on February 22, 1981, when the Stastny brothers were playing for the Quebec Nordiques against the Capitals in Washington. Peter had four goals and four assists, and Anton had three goals and five assists in the 11-7 Quebec victory. Ironically, the Statsnys are Slovaks playing for a Canadian team in the U.S. capital on George Washington's birthday.

## BILL STEWART

THE ONLY INDIVIDUAL to serve as a major league baseball umpire, an NHL referee, and the coach of a Stanley Cup champion.

Bill Stewart was an umpire in the National League and a referee in the NHL when he was hired to coach the Chicago Blackhawks for the 1937-38 season. Chicago had only a 14-25-9 regular-season record, but stunned everyone by winning the Stanley Cup. Stewart was fired the next season midway through a 12-28-8 season and returned to his duties as a referee. Stewart was an NHL referee for nine seasons and an umpire in the National League for 22 years.

## JIM STEWART

THE ONLY GOALTENDER to allow five goals in his only period in an NHL game.

In perhaps the worst performance by a man in a mask since Adam West played Batman, Jim Stewart of the Boston Bruins played only one period in his NHL career and allowed five goals on just nine shots. It happened on January 10, 1980, against the St. Louis Blues at the Boston Garden. Stewart was called up from Utica in the Eastern League and drew the start because of injuries to both of Boston's regular goalies. Stewart allowed goals on three of the first four shots he faced in 3:46, for a 7-4 loss.

## NELS STEWART

THE ONLY PLAYER to score two goals in a four-second span.

Nels Stewart scored the two quickest goals by one individual in NHL history on January 3, 1931, for the Montreal Maroons in a 5-3 win over the Boston Bruins in Montreal. Stewart scored at 8:24 and 8:28 of the third period, which helped Montreal overcome a 3-1 deficit in the final 20 minutes of play.

## St. Louis Blues

THE ONLY TEAM to be swept in the Stanley Cup finals three years in a row.

Entering the league as an expansion franchise in 1967-68, the St. Louis Blues reached the Stanley Cup finals during the first three years of their existence, but once there failed to win a game. In 1968 and 1969, they were swept by the Montreal Canadiens and in 1970 by the Boston Bruins.

## Patrik Sundstrom

THE ONLY PLAYER with three goals and five assists in a Stanley Cup game.

Patrik Sundstrom was on fire for the New Jersey Devils against the Washington Capitals in a play-off game on April 22, 1988, in East Rutherford. He had three goals and five assists as New Jersey rolled to a 10-4 win. Mark Johnson, a member of the 1980 U.S. gold medal Olympic hockey team, scored goals on four of Sundstrom's assists.

## Louis and Grace Sutter

THE ONLY COUPLE to produce six sons who played in the NHL.

Louis and Grace Sutter of Viking, Alberta, produced six sons who appeared in an NHL uniform. Brent, who debuted in 1980-81, and twins Rich and Ron, who were both rookies in 1982-83, were active in the league in the 1993-94 season. Brian played from 1976-77 through 1987-88, Duane from 1979-80 until 1989-90, and Darryl from 1979-80 through 1986-87. Through the 1992-93 season, the six Sutters had scored 1,233 goals in the NHL. For five seasons (1982-83 to 1986-87) all six were in the league at the same time.

## JEAN-GUY TALBOT

THE ONLY COACH whose team allowed five goals in two minutes and seven seconds.

Jean-Guy Talbot's St. Louis Blues allowed the five fastest goals in history to the Pittsburgh Penguins on November 22, 1972, in Pittsburgh. The Penguins scored five goals by five different players in a two-minute, seven-second span of the third period on their way to a 10-4 win. The goals were scored by Bryan Hextall at 12:00, Jean Pronovost at 12:18, Al McDonough at 13:40, Ken Schinkel at 13:49, and Ron Schock at 14:07.

## Rick Tocchet

THE ONLY PLAYER with over 100 points and 250 penalty minutes in the same season.

Rick Tocchet managed to find both the net and the penalty box with regularity during the 1992-93 season with the Pittsburgh Penguins. He had 109 points, on 48 goals and 61 assists, and accumulated 252 penalty minutes.

## Bryan Trottier

THE ONLY PLAYER with six points in one period.

Bryan Trottier set a league record for most points in one period with six on three goals and three assists for the New York Islanders against the New York Rangers on December 23, 1978, on Long Island. Trottier also scored goals in the first and third periods to give him five goals and eight points in the game, as the Islanders rolled to a 9-4 win.

## Norm Ullman

THE ONLY PLAYER to score two goals within five seconds of each other in a Stanley Cup play-off game.

Norm Ullman scored the two quickest goals in Stanley Cup history for the Detroit Red Wings on April 11, 1965, against the Chicago Blackhawks and goaltender Glenn Hall in Detroit. The goals came at 17:35 and 17:40 of the second period and lifted the Red Wings from a 2-1 deficit to a 3-2 lead. The Red Wings won 4-2 and took a 3-2 lead in the best-of-seven series. Chicago came back and won the series in seven games, however.

## Vancouver Canucks

THE ONLY NHL team to suffer through 15 consecutive losing seasons.

The Vancouver Canucks entered the NHL as an expansion team in 1970-71 and had a losing record for 19 of its first 21 seasons, including 15 in a row from 1976-77 through 1990-91. The Canucks did reach the Stanley Cup finals in 1981-82, however, after a 30-33-17 regular season. In the finals, Vancouver was swept four straight by the New York Islanders.

## Dennis Ververgaert

THE ONLY PLAYER to score twice in a 10-second span in an All-Star Game.

Dennis Ververgaert of the Vancouver Canucks scored twice in a 10-second span for the Campbell Conference in the All-Star Game on January 20, 1976, in Philadelphia. Ververgaert tallied at 4:33 and 4:43 of the third period, but the Wales Conference prevailed 7-5.

## GEORGES VEZINA

THE ONLY GOALTENDER with a play-off winning percentage over .750.

During his outstanding career in goal with the Montreal Canadiens from 1917 through 1926, Georges Vezina had a play-off record of 19 wins and six losses for a winning percentage of .760. The father of 22 children, Vezina died at the age of 39 from tuberculosis, just four months after playing in his last NHL game. The Vezina Trophy, awarded each year to the best goaltender in the NHL, is named in his honor.

## Washington Capitals

THE ONLY TEAM to lose 17 games in a row.

The Washington Capitals lost a record 17 games in a row in 1974-75 as a first-year expansion team. The streak began on February 18 and ended on March 28 with a 5-3 win over the California Golden Seals in Oakland. The Capitals finished the season with a record of 8-67-5. The Capitals also allowed a record 446 goals during the campaign.

## Ed Westfall

THE ONLY COACH to win seven straight games in one year in the play-offs while facing elimination.

Ed Westfall's New York Islanders reached the play-offs for the first time in 1974-75 with a 33-25-22 record, and made an immediate impact. In the quarterfinals, the Islanders trailed the Pittsburgh Penguins in games 3-0, then rallied to win four in a row to take the series. In the semifinals, the Islanders again lost the first three games, but won the next three to force a seventh game. The Cinderella story ended in a 4-1 loss in Philadelphia.

## Dave "Tiger" Williams

THE ONLY PLAYER to total more than 3,500 penalty minutes in a career.

Dave "Tiger" Williams became very acquainted with the penalty box during his NHL career. With the Toronto Maple Leafs, Vancouver Canucks, Detroit Red Wings, Los Angeles Kings, and Hartford Whalers from 1974-75 through 1987-88, Williams totaled 3,966 minutes in penalties. A left wing, he had 241 goals and 272 assists.

## Dunc Wilson

THE ONLY GOALTENDER to allow three goals in 20 seconds.

Vancouver Canucks goaltender Dunc Wilson allowed three Bruins goals in a 20-second stretch of the third period in an 8-3 loss at the Boston Garden on February 25, 1971. With the score 2-2, the tie was broken in a flourish on goals by John Bucyk at 4:50, Ed Westfall at 5:02, and Ted Green at 5:10.

## Winnipeg Jets

THE ONLY TEAM to go 30 games without a win.

The 1980-81 Winnipeg Jets went 30 games without a victory, which broke the record of 27 set by the 1975-76 Kansas City Scouts. During the streak, which lasted from October 19 until December 20, the Jets lost 23 and tied seven. It finally ended on December 23 in a 5-4 win over the Colorado Rockies in Winnipeg when Willy Lindstrom scored the tie-breaking goal at 18:10 of the third period. The Jets finished the season with a 9-57-14 record.

## LORNE "GUMP" WORSLEY

THE ONLY GOALTENDER to be credited with 353 losses in a career.

Lorne "Gump" Worsley had a career record of 335-353-150 because he was stuck on some bad and mediocre clubs with the New York Rangers from 1952 through 1963 and with the Minnesota North Stars from 1969 until his retirement in 1974. In between his years in New York and Minnesota, however, Worsley had a chance for some glory with the Montreal Canadiens. He played on four Stanley Cup champions, and was a second-team All-Star in 1965-66 and a first-team All-Star in 1967-68.

John S. Snyder is a sportswriter and the author of five other books for Chronicle Books: *Play Ball!* (1991), *Touchdown!* (1992), *Tennis!* (1993), *Basketball!* (1993), and *Goal!* (1994). He also co-authored *Day-by-Day in Cincinnati Bengals History* and *Day-by-Day in Cincinnati Reds History.* He lives in Cincinnati.

Mike Harling (Introduction) owns Sportsbook Plus in Vancouver. He is an avid hockey fan.